uncharted territory
lifeboat
you, me, and the big blue sea
captain's coming

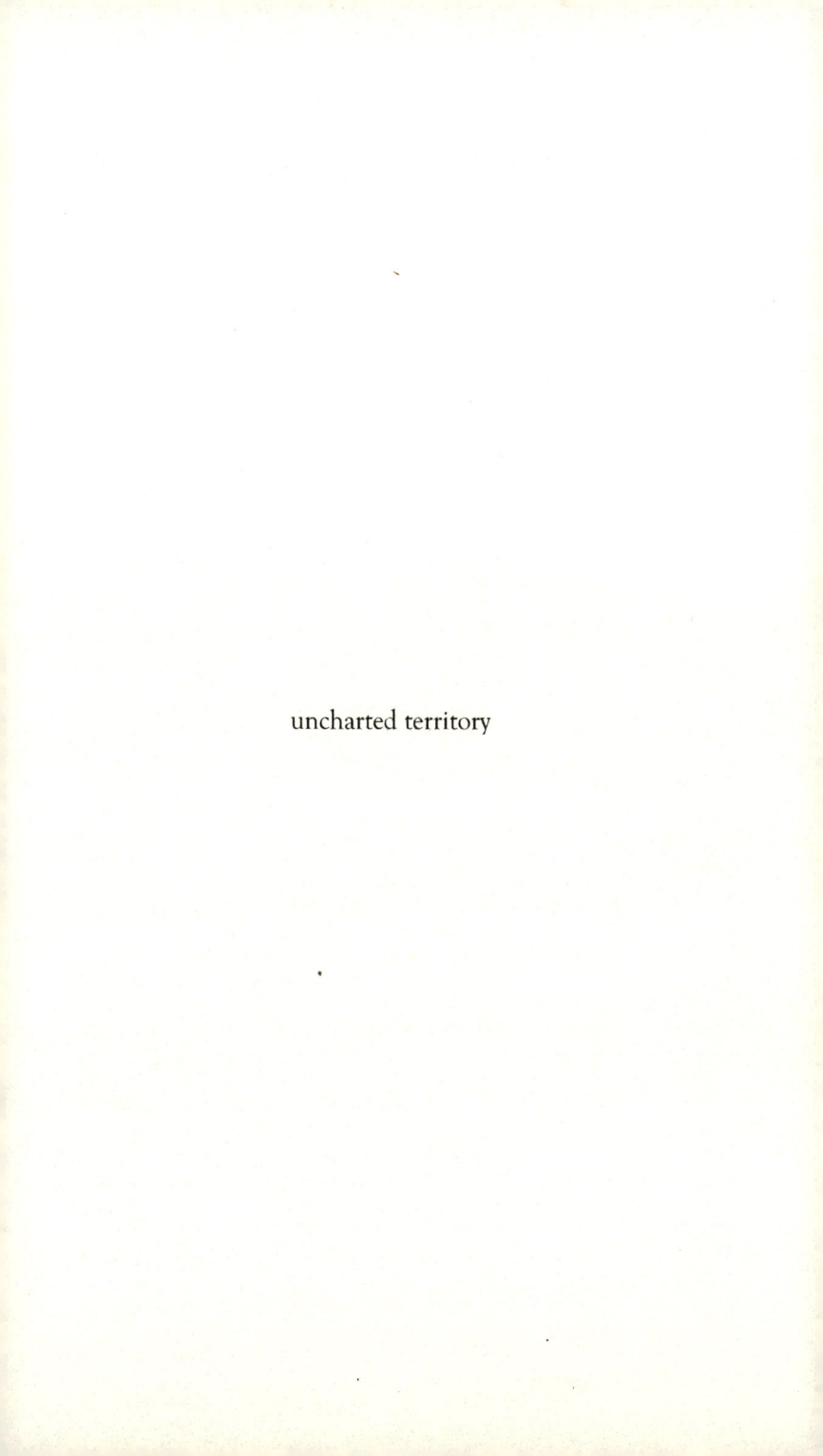

uncharted territory

so this is the new normal.
it doesn't always start with change
and change does not always come in the form of a loss,
but it surely feels like it does.
i don't know what the future holds.
i'm not sure of anything except that
if life is changing for me,
it is changing for those closest to me too.
and that is a consolation and an indifference.

one day you stopped smiling and i lost sight of the moon.

when the tide quickly changes,
what a thing it is to grieve
what you do not want to grieve.
to not grieve at all because you can't.
to hold on to hope when it feels like
everyone around you wants to move on and has.
as if this reality is really that black and white.

you're consumed.
consumed with the search for the truth.
you become distant.
you need something, someone.
a voice of reason you won't listen to.
you say "here.
you wear the glow as i cannot."

what happens when the truth was
never what you were looking for?
you were looking for what to do with that truth
when you found it.
a purpose.
now that it has come to an end,
who are you?

you were born with a body full of water
to fill and cleanse yourself.
still, you don't see it as enough.
still, the first place you look for love
is everywhere but inside you.

as more meaning comes into your life,
everything you read or see will
breathe different.

before you begin your exploration,
know you will get lost.
it's an inevitable given.
you might not get lost in the way you think,
but you will get lost.
there are so many ways to go off-course.
losing your sense of direction-
(don't forget a compass.)
losing your sense of purpose-
(here comes an existential crisis.)
one too many in a crowded room-
(being invisible.)
i just hope when the time comes you embrace it.

one day you'll know these words were for you,
and it'll make them that much *sweeter*.

tonight, pretend no one has mapped the moon.
become an astronomer, find the truth.
it is harmful to describe things
based on how they appear.
the moon has always known
its dark spots were not water.

when you love them it's okay to ask,
"is this appropriate? is this right?"

and when you love them through their mourning,
as they are close-mouthed and tight-lipped,
remain at a distance, but don't forget to check-in.
remember far does not mean dark,
silence does not mean void,
and not every light that glows is gold.

it doesn't mean you are ungrateful.
if you leave a good life to search for a better one.

even submerged in water,
plants do their part.
though delicate,
they give balance to the pond,
absorbing what is harmful
for it to maintain existence.
some drift away and regrow.
some drift away and go home.
but it was for the greater good,
the greater good,
the greater good.
and though it might never see it,
come out of the other side,
it believes.
and knowing that there is
no breath too small,
it gives it.

i have this job from 9-5.
you have this job from 9-5.
i think yours is from 9-5.
i see you each day a little before 9.
i wonder if it's a job you like.
are you miserable like me from 9-5?
maybe you could find something you don't mind
if you weren't like me from 9-5.

do you remember finding the
taraxacum erythrospermum flower
when we were kids?
you know the one we could destroy with a touch,
that felt like feathers against our fingers
and looked like snow?
they were everywhere then–
even when we didn't need to make a wish.
i haven't seen one since.
i haven't seen one since.

i don't think i was ever told why we wished on them.
it was something all the little children did.
legend has it, if you blow it off in one breath,
the person you love will love you back.
if it takes more than one try, they have qualms.
or whoever engages in the act will have
thoughts and dreams carried to loved ones.

there is something so beautiful about
hopes flying away.
to bloom elsewhere,
up to five feet away.
how i wish for that again and some
wind beneath my shoe.
maybe all the dandelions i blew
were preparing me to find you.

i have no idea what you look like
but i know you are dreaming of me too.

here is what i know of love: it is full of maybes.
maybes and dreams like maybe you'll find me.
maybe when you do you'll tell me you like me
better with my hair down.
you won't care that you can't tell
the difference between real and realesque.
you'd want whatever makes me happy.
whatever makes me feel more like me.
you won't point out that i look different
without lipstick.
you'd remind me that i'm beautiful
even when i know i am, and
i'd plead ignorance just to hear it again.

the mind plays tricks and you're some kind of *magic*.

you know as well as i that pain isn't always instant.
i'm not talking about the pain from a great injury.
more like the pain you feel after days of not noticing.
like washing your hands after a thin cut,
or the pain you feel from losing someone suddenly,
but not having it register until you do something that
you used to do with them and now no longer can.

i know the reason why
it doesn't go immediately dark after sunset.
the rays linger in the air and reflect off
water vapor and dust particles.
hope prolonging.
and the consolation is we're in this together.
through the dark.

at 10 am you woke up to rain
& became a turtle in a shell.
got up, poured coffee. perhaps sat
by the window in your room and
watched the water beads drop.
on your nightstand is a book
you haven't touched.
you turn the page.

when you look out the window,
the rain has gone just like the day.
sometimes stillness and silence is
all you'll have energy for
and <u>that's okay</u>.

how do i test the thickness of
the ice around your heart?
formed from a cold winter of a past love.
would you let me get near it?
make a small puncture and
stick a measuring tape inside?
get a reading?
they say 4 inches is safe enough to walk,
but i know to proceed with caution.
how do i test the thickness of
the ice around your heart?
will it be like this all season?
even if it was safe enough to walk,
would you let me?
this is new territory for the both of us.
how do i test the thickness of
the ice around your heart?
i can imagine you're scared.
tell me so when i eventually move,
we both don't
fall through.

you wonder if it is wrong of you.
not wanting to be touched unless
it is initiated or accepted by you first.
if it is a predecessor to your love life in the future
when you are afraid to have sex but want to have sex.
you wonder if there will come a time when it feels right.

you are a sunrise.
sunsets are my favorite,
but there are some sunrises
too beautiful not to name.

someday, i will be a mother.
and with everything i know,
and how i am now,
i wonder if i will be a good one.
there is so much going on in the world,
not to mention the things going on inside of me.
would it be unmotherly to bring a child into this world
when hatred grows where flowers should be?
will i grow out of not wanting to be touched
or will that remain like everything else?
i know i have years to go.
haven't had my second kiss or first breakup.
but these are things that fill my brain
and i'm not sure i want to stop thinking of them.

all i hear are birds chirping in the morning
and crickets chirping at night,
and all i can think about is how maybe, someday,
i can wake up to something like this and
be kept awake by someone like you.

i'm thinking of the future again.
this time i am thinking of who out of my siblings
will take care of my mother when
she can no longer care for herself.
right now, my mother's mother is sitting in a room
surrounded by people from all walks of life.
whose ailments range in degree from
physical to mental instability.
i see what it is for my mom to care for my grandma.
a single mom of four, caring for five.
six, if you include her.
every day she'll clock off work and drive an hour
to the facility to give her medicine and
take her to the lavatory.
sure, there are nurses for that,
but most have said it's not their ward
or make her wait or leave her places
to have her find her way when she's old and weak.
it made me realize that there's no way around it.
one day you'll need someone to
be an advocate for you.
that's the way of this world.
so i'm thinking of the future again.
and though i don't have all the answers now,
i know if i did, they'd probably change.

if you kiss me, kiss me twice.
once to remember how it feels like to be kissed,
and twice to remember how it feels like to be kissed by

you.

have you ever seen the sunrise through window blinds?
a subtle pink and a subtle orange.
the sunset on office buildings
a royal purple.
no shades, just a glow.
you knew something magnificent was about to happen.
all you had to do was look.
good things are everywhere waiting for us to see them.

you are the words i say but can never hold.
you are the air i feel but can never see.
you are everything and everywhere but never beside me.

the fastest healing property,
my tongue is all too forgiving.
more than ever it wants, like the way
"the heart wants what the heart wants."
it's so demanding this feeling.
beyond my control.
and just for a moment, i want you to know /
the second you left that one time we fought /
all i wanted to do was kiss and makeup.

does anybody care about the stars anymore?
it bothers me that they can be seen so prominently
in some places and not in others.
that whenever there's a meteor shower,
i'd have a better chance of seeing it if
i was on a different plane.

if this is how we treat real stars,
neglectful because light is all around us;
street lights, buildings, and cars.
imagine how we treat the ones inside of us.
how brightly would we shine if
we turned off all that luster?
and does anybody care to know?

my friends say
i should ask what we are
but i do not want to know.
the devil is in the details and
i want to dance with the angels
a bit longer.

today i'm posting a help wanted sign.
i don't know if anyone reads the paper
but i've tried everything else thus far.
post lamps, abandoned buildings, dog parks.
no answer.
perhaps people want to know
the face behind who they're helping.
would it help if i told you that my face is
tear stricken, tired, and worn,
and i do not know how to go on?
that's no big secret.
not even close.
the truth is you're just like me.
you just hide that the most.

before we call it Spring, flowers are already blooming.
so many things happen before we name them.

think fresco painting-
Adam's finger and then God's,
not touching.
50-60 megaparsecs or 163-261 light-years
of thread-like formation between their fingertips.
galaxy filaments showing the gaps
between Heaven & Earth.
acting as a liaison as life travels.
proof that there can be space between two people
and love at the same time.

the approaching night doesn't have to be a prison.
see it as a bridge.
you're at the cusp of magic.

you're free to roam.
fall in love, stay in love.
if you're truly daring,
you'll take your time on your way home.

the stories they tell are true you know.
walks in the park are good for the soul.

if you believe in loss, you believe in love.

you'll remember this like it was yesterday.
tomorrow came and with it fabric you did not ask for.
"cover yourself," it seemed to say.
the days will get cold and lonely.

you don't know a thing about sewing.
don't know how you survived this long.
but here you are standing,
pricking your fingers.
pricking your fingers
over and over.
bleeding just to make yourself a quilt.
you are going to get through this.

the pattern is this:
breathe, sleep, wake, bathe, eat, repeat
laced with whatever you've been doing
and what you can do now.
the only difference is a change in scenery.

i know it's hard.
i miss people too.
but the energy they filled you with
you must now harness for yourself
from yourself.
it's the most powerful energy of them all.

my favorite passage of time-
the horizon of the sky and the ocean,
the spread of sunset in waves,
the anticipation that lines my whole body
when you lean in to kiss me.

before it goes dark completely,
your sight goes before your hearing,
open arms fold,
the sun caresses all things below
without touching it,
and it is a slow descent.
something resembling hope peers over
like shameful eyes above a cover.
a man at work turns out the light
and turns away from his desk.
a baby cries.

at first, your fear will be stronger than your regret
but then your regret will be stronger than your fear.

as you do when you are leaving any place
for an extended period of time,
you draw the blinds.
you draw the blinds, tidy the rooms,
make the beds, sweep the floors,
dust the mirrors, and restore everything
to its former glory.
nothing has changed except
everything has changed.
the difference is now it's furnished.
with decor and memories and smells
you can't carry with you
and yet still carry the thought.
there are so many things to think about knowing
your body is a home.
you wish you thought that much about you.

i mostly drink tea on sick days,
but if i had to for any other reason,
how poetic would it be if i brewed my own
so i could take the tea leaves and
try to tell the future of you and me
as if i believed in such things.

in a world where you are here, i am
the "elephant of the house."
all of us combined- three siblings, a grandmother, and you,
equals me.

the last time i saw an elephant was in the eighth grade.
maybe there was a time after that, when i first went to the zoo,
but that's not the story i'm telling here.

in a world where you are here, it's no wonder why
i don't love my body. i told you i'm not into scales and
you talk about the things i watch and read affecting my brain
as if i'm not old enough to make a decision for myself.
you say i'm afraid of the number i'll see when the truth is
i could step on a scale if i wanted to but now
i just couldn't really care.

what i am is not a number.
what i am is immeasurable.
just for a moment, i want to talk about science.
i'll never know how many star ashes i can't see make up part of me
though i know i am two-thirds water. did you know we are also
65% oxygen? if it wasn't for this, i don't know how i would be able to
breathe because your repetition takes the life out of me,
the kindness out of me,
the love out of me.

believing this will be my greatest triumph
and then you'll never hear from me:
mirror, mirror on the wall,
scale, scale on the floor,
you have no power over me.

we were dark and light.
heat and cool.
you absorbed me,
and i reflected you.

dude wants to know my history.
i'm hesitant to give it.
my mouth is nothing but magic phrases.
he'll disappear. they always do.
i give him the benefit of the doubt.
"what do you want to know?"
he asks me about preferences.
"i'm not sure." "i don't know."
dude presses on. i have to give eventually.
eventually becomes now because
i've never been good at lying.
"i've never been in a relationship before."
abracadabra, abracadabra.
dude presses on.
open sesame.
"i'm not allowed to date," i say.
"never been kissed."
dude doesn't think it's cute,
tell me there's no shame.
doesn't fight for me,
doesn't know how i feel.
my life is a raging sea but
he isn't the only one that gets
caught in the storm.

if they give you all the reasons to stay,
perhaps that is the reason to run away.
for they have thought about it coming down
to this and there is no excuse for
the way they behaved.

at times i feel
i have made a menagerie of my heart.
there are lovers instead of lions,
most with blue eyes, some with manes,
but no matter. i loved them all the same.
i tell the story of us.
that's what all new lovers want to know.
how we met, what we did, how we ended.
i seem to have become a zookeeper
but i'm not too fond of the zoo.
they ask why i can't let go.
i tell them what could have been is
hard to tame.

they say i'm in my head and my head is full of you.

remember when we were young
and how falling asleep under the canary sun was
the most of our worries?

how our parents told us to count sheep or stars
and when we finally woke up we could never remember
the last number of stars or sheep we counted-reached.

remember the secrets and inside jokes they kept
or the things we could never have
and how they said they'll tell us or we'll get them
when we're older and it felt like we would never get older?
- we got there, we are there

what do you want to be when you grow up?
what did you major in?
what are you doing, where are you now?
- nothing, nowhere

go to church. pray. find a job, find a partner.
time is ticking, time is running,
time is an astronaut gravity cannot hold down.

the first thing i do when i come across a man is
look at his hand;

and the wolf at my throat is me.

you should know i sleep with the covers off
and somehow manage to find myself under them
again and again.
in a perfect world, this is a metaphor for how i love.
i think i let go, but when things end,
i always try to bring them back from the dead.

i had you go on believing because it was easier to see you smile
and not know what i know. it was easier for me to
leave.

when you're far out at sea,
and the waters are deep,
and the sky is perfectly dark,
how do you navigate the ocean?
when you're hiking through forest,
and you haven't got a compass,
how do you stay true north?
when the lights go out,
as often they do,
who do you turn to?
it is you?
and is it true the good we do,
the prayers we say,
are stored up in a bank
to aid us on a rainy day?

it's draining, isn't it?
trying to love someone who doesn't love you.
but flowers will never bloom in the wrong soil.

mother, i am wondering if you hear me.
wondering how my light can be your light
because you wish it to be so,
and yet, it is too quiet, too short, too young
to reach you.
wondering how we are of the same wave
and different wavelengths.

i owe you thanks for instilling in me
the value of education.

in middle school,
i would see posters saying
"no child gets left behind,"
but it was always your emphasis of
"knowledge is power."
"knowledge is power."
that spurred me on.

because of you,
i focused on education instead of boys,
and i don't resent you for that,
but i can't help but wonder how different
my life would be if that was a decision
i made by my own choice.
how different i would have turned out if
you taught me i could have had both.

he left and there are questions i dare not ask.
is she strict because she loves me
or is she strict because she wants me to love myself?

it's hard to say,
but maybe once upon a time
you told me not to grow up too fast,
and i wish i knew how to tell you to
because you wanted to play games
and house wasn't one of them.

i. underneath the incandescence,
scars bear birth to a collapse
through thoughts transmitted in synapse.
(insert self-criticism here)
a nebula of dust, hydrogen, helium,
and other elements become dense.
you yearn to convert the energy into love
and become a friend to the dark.

ii. a wolf howls at the moon and you condemn yourself
for being invisible to the naked eye.
wanting to be just as *bright*.

although it rains freshwater,
the oceans will always be salt.
no matter how much we crave change,
some things are just meant to be as they are.

the only pants you put on today were the ones
society told you to. they don't stretch or give you room to
breathe but you wear them anyway because it's the "right thing."
you keep your head down because small talk triggers you.
the answer always is "you're not okay but you're trying to be."
there was no question asked, but there should have been.
most times you don't know what you want, but you want to be
understood. curious how when you express yourself, people
decide they're experts on what is. after this, you will go home, eat,
sleep - feed your body. you will take off those pants and forget to do
something for your mind.

people say speak from the heart but
that's easy to do on paper.
when the time comes and
we're face to face with the one we love,
alone in a room with only our light,
that's the one thing that
fails us.

these days we sit like
bumper cars facing each other
and our thoughts are the driver.
one is at a standstill.
one is already heated up.
one has already given up.
and one is already driving.

it is okay if you are still taking time
to figure yourself out.
you might be a home that
you've lived in since birth,
but that doesn't mean you can't
stub your toe in the dark.

you never admit you're wrong.
there's always a clause,
and i'm too not young to believe.

you say if i am wrong, then let me be wrong.
code for still do it your way.
i do, but i make a habit to gift
question after question.

the yelling comes after.
my ask has never been about you,
but that's all you make it out to be.

i know you'd never lead me astray,
but i'm no sheep,
and i haven't quite figured out yet
how to quiet my voice
in a way that shows you
this path is for me.

we are so similar and you are so easy to talk to and
that's no reason to wish you were mine but i do.

- i love you and you forget i'm human

we stopped playing games when we were younger,
but we still go around in circles.
always with our answers,
but the world tells us to give it to them straight.
when you've been devoid of a thing for so long,
how do you let go?
when you had to swallow your words
when you had so much to say,
how do you not spit it back up?

there is so much going on but
you can still buy into this story:
you are going to be okay.

tectonic plates are shifting within you.
volcanic activity, mountains, earthquakes, & trenches
form along its edges.
you should not feel sorry
or apologize for your discord
when wars have been raging inside you.

living with depression is like living as a landlocked pebble
waiting for a sea that might never come.

- you want to move but you can't.

once in the evening hours
i took a mason jar from my kitchen.
purple in color, medium in size.
i went outside where the air was warm;
towards the lot in search of glow bugs.

i must have held out my hand to try and catch one.
wondered why God created something
so small that some aren't even awake
to see.

but then i thought,
"all fireflies must feel insignificant
until they light up the night."

blooming does not mean your petals are ready to open,
doesn't mean that they are ready to see you,
doesn't mean that you are ready to be seen.

you only color inside the lines
when you're handed pen and paper
in preschool, at the age of four,
when your body doesn't know to move
just wrist and finger in opposed to most of you,
and you're trying to develop control.

you only color outside the lines
when you're handed pen and paper
in the comfort of your home and mama says,
"it's okay to cross the border.
let your imagination run wild-
as long as you make the life you dream
come alive."

when home gets hard and lines become people
and paper becomes maps and pen becomes bags
and think big becomes the American dream,
how do we turn our backs on
the children inside of us?

it takes light from the sun
8 minutes and 30 seconds
to reach us.
when it does,
we are not seeing the Sun
as it is now, but
as it was.
we are not seeing each other
as we are now,
but as we were.

i. you were never taught how to pack a suitcase.
it has always been innate after you've learned how to fold
your first clean set of clothes.
sleeves go in, bring down the neck.
it's *neater* that way.

ii. society has taught you to be healthy is to be skinny.
more of this, less of that.
once in a while you fold yourself to make more room.
there is never enough room.

iii. you spend your days over porcelain sink
sticking a finger or two down your throat.

if anyone asks, you're going on a trip.
the beach, perhaps.

iv. don't you know the only trip you are packing for
is a trip out of you and you are not a suitcase?

they can make you want to be a better person, but
know who you are if they leave.

the sun rose and
it is not a lover because it gifts us light.
it is a lover because it gifts us thorns.
and i know it's tiring bleeding
on the promise of "i'll keep waiting"
and "i'll keep going,"
but the sun rises knowing
that its journey through the sky
is not the same,
and its color lives in you.
i wish you could see how
sun-kissed you are.
how Heaven opens up for you.
how it's a beautiful thing
to have a friend in this forever,
if you choose.

there is a world that my lungs will never forget
because it has yet to remember and
i am done waiting for it.

what a time to be alive and bury their name in your soul.
tell only stories you and they know.
what a time to be alive and see a fossil up close.
you got through pain and so much more.
what a time to be alive and wonder and wander.
it's a new season but a tale as old as you.
there is much to unravel.
much you can't explain.
but if you were asked, you would do it all again.
what a time to be alive.

lifeboat

thank you.
for teaching me how to be everything
so that i lack nothing.

the first time you went out to sea
you were eager to rejoin the water.
perhaps you were going fishing.
you learned the best time of day is
early morning or late evening.
a day without much wind,
one hour before or after high or low tides.
between new moons and full.
you learned how to hook a needle and the bait.
you wore a lifejacket, learned how to steer a lifeboat.
and then you learned to fish.
learned how to call things to you when you want it.
learned you won't always get what you want.
that life is a life of waiting.

the water fighting to keep you gone
is the same water that can fight to keep you alive.
learn how to channel the waves.

what holds you when you need it?
is it your mother's touch?
your father's or your lovers?
is it your work; the hope you find in it?
your faith?
the words you've read, the words you've made?
what holds you when you need it?
what carries you to shore?
what steers the oars in you
when you find you can't go on no more?
what holds you when you need it?
find the common denominator.
the root of all is kindness.
the kindness lives in you.
what holds you when you need it?
write it down, make a list.
crumple it, set it on fire, give it to the wind.
when all is said and done, don't forget to breathe it in.
what holds you when you need it?
answer me that.
answer me that and you'll find you're not alone.

what a strength it is to believe in yourself
and live that every day.

the clouds gave into the sky,
broke and fell into the earth as rain,
and ended up back in the clouds
to fall and stay as something else.

- it is not too late to pursue your dreams

as long as
you have light,
you have energy.
find the light.
bask in it.
never let it go.

on the days you feel
the sadness lingering like a ghost
and everything is sudden and back to back,
acknowledge that it is real but remind yourself that
you are still here.
welcome the ghost in like an old friend.
ask what you can do for it,
or better yet, what it can do for you.
if it needs to relay a message,
tell it it's come to the right place.
open all the windows,
boil some water in a kettle for tea.
listen to it tell you how the other side is dark
and nothing looks familiar,
but if you reach out your hand,
a hand reaches back.
remember the good times as you thank it for its time,
and watch it enter the light.

too much weight,
you drown.
too little weight,
you sink.
just enough,
you *float*.

so this is how you predict rain:
achy bones - weak knees,
halos around the moon.
rainbows in the morning
& no sign of dew.

smoke clouds,
buttermilk clouds,
richness in the earth.
wind sails & red skies,
lowly swooping birds.

lick the tip of your finger.
put it to the air.
take it all to heart,
just don't give up.

so the future is nebulous,
and salt won't heal these wounds,
there is evidence that your body tells you
when certain weather is approaching,
and someday, i promise, it'll be good.

find what leaves you lighter than before.

according to science,
we emit a light that our human eyes cannot see,
but if this is true then how do i see the light in everything?
i see you shine in the sun,
i see you shine through your kindness,
i see you shine with my eyes closed.
i always believed you are at your brightest
in your darkest moments.
i don't need science to tell me that
but maybe you
do.

say ashes are stars.
when i die i want you to scatter mine over parking lots.
give the roads a piece of me and i'll guide you home.

there are days where it won't always feel like
you are chasing your own tail.
on those days don't ask where you are going
when you're going or who will return you
to the earth when you get there.
personify the love and make it last.
even when you know that
the loss will become real. greater.
because once you're gone
it won't be the same as when you left.
so are you really returning as much as
coming home to something new?

all the rough patches
you're going through right now,
i hope you let them stay.
because one day you'll go through
a time tougher than this,
and you won't consider this a rough patch,
you'll consider it your *triumph*.

you got here and the grass wasn't as green,
the sky wasn't as blue, the water wasn't as clear
as you thought it would be.
the dreams you had are just that. dreams.
you haven't hit rock bottom but
you're not far from it either.
the more you think about it,
the more you think maybe you should have listened.
you've never been one to lean on opinions
but now you question everything.
you can't help but wonder-
maybe they were right.
but you're forgetting that you have tasted the sun
and the rain won't always be pouring.
the grass will be green, the sky will be blue,
the water will be clear just as you thought it would be.
and that little glimpse of sunshine will remind you of why
you began in the first place.

no matter where i hide,
light always finds me.
and if it can find me,
surely, surely
it can find you too.

when the day came you packed your bags.
you packed your bags and didn't look back.
there were many times you didn't know
where or who you were
and most days that fazed you.

i know.
i've been there too.
the trick is to:

breathe.
orient.
allow yourself to be where you are
to find where you are.

it *works.*
i'm telling you.

you are an infinite world of chances. just think:
one of your petals has the chance to bloom.

sometimes part of you wonders
what's the point of the sky when
you can't see the stars,
and what's the point of the stars when
there is also a sun,
and how you can say anything different.
in reply, say this:
the only star you're supposed to look at is
the one inside of you.
the size of your star doesn't diminish your light.
that suns blind and stars guide.
that everyone has doubts about
the way they've lived their life.
and too, even still,
it's not the same because it's not you.

if i could choose a superpower,
i would love to be your thoughts.
constant;
always reminding you
how beautiful you are.

when pieces of your life are in different places,
when everything seems to be going in the wrong direction,
when you're feeling small,
just know that even small particles can influence light.
that even light scatters. it scatters and looks like
purple skies with a multitude of clouds in sight and clean air.

- so breathe. your time will appear.

ask yourself why the heart is in a ribcage
and you'll know why your heart will never leave you
even if they do.

if there ever comes a time when you need to
focus on anything else,
think of how you can see the sunset on your way home
when you get off work
before the dead of winter.
or listen to the song you know will take you all the way there
when you get off the train.
listen to the rhythm of your heart.
your beautiful dear heart.
think of the life you could have someday.
think of the stars and how they shine.
think of romance, think of them.
think of you with them.
think of anything.
find loopholes.
no matter how hard it tries,
sadness can't resist beautiful simple things.
instead of coping, make room.

- you asked me how i cope. i said, "i don't."

if a star's age and origin can be determined
by its motion through space,
all the more reason to keep going.
remember how far you traveled to get here
and never let go of that light.

think to yourself
all of the secrets and surprising things
the ocean must carry.
and when the night comes and
you begin to doubt your purpose,
think of how the wood drifts and
see how it becomes a shelter.
see how it becomes food.
see how it becomes art.

by nature,
you will leave behind something beautiful.
turn to the seashells
whenever you feel you have nothing to give
to the world when you're gone.
their stories echo for us to hear.

and then it starts.
the crying, the sniffling.
the headache from thinking too much about something sad.
the desire to hold it all in and tell yourself you can do it.
but that makes it worse and you cry on.

sometimes you wonder what it would be like to die
and what the easiest way would be.
you suck in deep and hold.
then releasing it more quickly than you held it in,
you double over, telling yourself you can't do it,
what were you thinking?

what tells you you're alive is
every emotion that courses through your veins.
what tells you you're alive is
your thoughts.
what tells you you're alive is
every situation that makes you feel like
you are drowning.
a lot of things tell you you're alive.
but the most important one is
the will you have to go *on*.

you, me, and the big blue sea

only you could
find a way
for both of us
to share our light
and not drown in it.

- for Michael Bagley, 1993-2016

"move," they say. "you are not a tree."
but it is because of the trees i breathe.
"brighten up," they say. "there is no reason to be blue."
but you cannot remove the ocean from man.
"i give up," they say. "i can't help the helpless."
but the moon never allowed waters to just be.

the ocean gives constantly and it is not any less of an ocean.

tabula rasa: a conversation

"how do you do it? how do you breathe when it pours & you feel flooded?"

"when it rains into an ocean, what happens?"

"it floods onto a neighboring surface."

"and what was the nature of that surface?"

"unflooded."

"you see, if it rains into an ocean, and it didn't come flooded, it won't remain flooded."

you are made of atoms
and you
matter.

your story is not a song that can be played by ear.
it is full of holds, suspensions.
intricate notes, softness & hardness.
strings & hammers.

people will try to pin you down to certain keys and pedals
and say this is who you are.
but you've always been more.
you are more.

the stars burned brighter when you were born
and each time you turn they are surely smiling.

- i want to find where they are and thank them

one night the light in my room went out
and my mom taught me to never touch
a light bulb with my bare hands,
for i am skin oil and salt,
and for every action, there is a reaction.
flickering & failing
and sometimes you won't see the flicker.
one night the light in my room went out
and i learned it is not better
to ask for forgiveness than permission,
because the light can go out in another person
and there's nothing you can do to bring it back.

as writers, we are told to never assume that
our readers will understand,
and i'm sure this is why i leave out nothing,
and give away everything in poetry, love, and life.

shape & size.
we used to fit together and soar endlessly
like a wooden airplane we put together when we were kids,
but now you're hell-bent out of shape.

our clothes used to be intermingled
in our vast closet with no doors,
but now yours are hidden at the back,
behind where the wall meets space.

funny how things as tiny as these,
can amount to the size of
a great barrier reef.

the rain has stopped but i still hear its patter.
it drips from bareness into a small pothole,
and i think from this i know what it means
to be full when empty for it is how you left me.

another word for heartache:

a. if i were to write a crossword, my first clue would be "another word for heartache" and i'd think about you. i'd look up the history of the crossword just to pass more time. did you know solutions must match their clues in terms of tense? for example, if the clue was "had already sung," the answer would be sang, not sing. i'd pretend not to know the answer and write down all the synonyms. pain. hurt. agony. sorrow. anguish. grief. affliction. i'd narrow it down based on space, but i'd still want to write "you."

b. for a second i'd like to talk about affliction. the reality is you are something that causes hurt but you are not the hurt. heartache doesn't stem from the person your heart aches about. heartache stems from the way they make you or made you feel. heartache stems from the emptiness of presence.

c. have you noticed on the really sad days there is much to feel and not much to say, and on the really happy days there is much to say and not much to feel? curious, isn't it? that joy does not know heartache's range.

we move in lovely ways. even our bones cry, *stay*.

when you come to my home
you will never see my father.
the dictionary defines home as
the place where one lives permanently,
especially as a member of a household or family.
we grow up with these ideas that family is
a mother, father, son, or daughter, living in
a space that was bought or even borrowed.
but if these things are true then
family and home were never meant for me.
and if that's one thing i learned then
i don't regret anything.
home is never a place that won't support you.
home is yourself, your ideas,
everything you've been through.
it is something that can shift, lift you up,
or even crumble.
for me, it is God, and myself, and my mother.
my brothers and sister,
a place i have lived in long.
it is the Earth and things that are to come.
it is love and light, love and light.
my name, and fond things i have been called.
the list goes on and on, and
my father might still be gone,
but it's okay because i am home and
that is enough for me.

like water, they are something you will retain.
the weight of them will reflect on you,
your face will be swollen with tears,
and you won't understand
how you were fine the first day
and worse the next.

the first problem with the term broken homes is
the word broken.
broken implies that what was can become again
and this broken is not a bone.
it cannot be x-rayed or snapped back into place.
if i show you my broken, it will never be exactly like yours.

the second problem with the term broken homes
is the term broken homes.
we are not from broken homes,
only a home that has been
broken into.
right before our eyes we watched
as they stole themselves from us,
but at the time we didn't know that's what was happening.
it's easy to make excuses for the people we love
and put their shortcomings on ourselves.
we feel responsible for the weight of our blood
and carry it as our own, but for how long?

how long will we shelve ourselves for them?
how long will we let them bite our hands?
how long, how long, how long?

i want to say that day you left
i wanted you to pull at my bones.
break them and take the short end
with you before you go
so i could stretch out my hand,
wish you to stay or come back.
but that day you left was a relief.
you pulled at my bones, breaking them,
taking the shorter end with you, and
i wished that i would get through this and
thanked God for being left with
the longer end.

we were taught to hide our time of month.
there's no need for you to know.
but what are we telling you other than
it's not easy being woman?

- after two periods there's no space

Saturdays were reserved for cleaning.
i brought out brooms instead of vacuums.
dusters and dirty laundry.
wood shined and the living room
smelled like citrus.

i've always liked the smell and taste of
acidic candy or fruits.
perhaps because i knew their word origin stemmed
from the language of romance.
did you know i am still sour at the thought of you?
i brought you into my home and now
i will never be able to sweep you under the rug
in a way that is forever.

a list of redundant truths:
- God made a place on this earth for me and you.
- "he who sings prays twice."
    - so even if you do, do not or don't yet believe,
      or lost faith for some reason, never stop singing.
      never stop letting them hear you.
      never stop fighting for what you believe in.
- you don't have to have faith to have hope.
(but wouldn't that be nice?)
- the Universe knows your heart.
sees your struggle.
calls your name.
- poetry has no rules.
breathe and never stop breathing.
tell the world how things make you feel.
- your favorite song should be the one you're in.
- what makes the many voices so beautiful,
aside from the fact that they are beautiful on their own,
is that they listen to each other.
- whatever you keep close, you'll attract in abundance.
- there is no shame in asking for help when
you need the support to bloom.

there is hope for you, little one.
you are a star.
burning,
vanishing,
always
returning.

you asked why can't we unwind the stars.
i said we can, but why should we?
if that was all we did, new stars would never be born.
we would miss out on so many things.
we would never look at the sky the same way.
maybe we would grow to resent that.
i would never want to.
i am too fond of the night.
too fond of you.
what i mean is, i love you.
but i consider this love a body of art,
and this loss does not define me.

we often mistake what we do as who we are,
but what we do can never be who we are,
who we are can be what we do.

you tell me i smell like outside.
i ask what does outside smell like?
you say, "grass."
i do not stop to think of
whether that is good or bad.
instead, i think of how many times
bees and flies have surrounded me.
joked, "it must have been my perfume"
as i swatted them away.
how many times did they consider me a friend
when i wore the color yellow?
how many times did i reject them?
how we are one with the earth-
are and will be dust.
i am sorry i wasn't a friend.
that i let my fear get in the way
of our sameness and oneness.
i hope you can forgive me
the next time i do it
again.

the more i love, the more there is to love.

the way you made love to me was art.
you were my first everything.
i was your first everything.
what we made you will make again with someone else,
but no matter the similarity, no two art pieces are the same.
i will always hold a special place in your heart.

- i am the love that made your love for her *better*

there is a time for telling stories
and we'll spend half our lives figuring out
the right times to tell them.
it is there at that moment
when we figure out when that
makes us an artist.

when all is quiet and i am left alone
in the twilight hours in this heavenly body,
all i can think about is endings.
ashes from ashes, dust to dust.
i think about the way i'll leave the earth
more than the state i'll be in when i leave it.
or the first of the firsts, the chosen ones,
that ate after being given everything.
had they not eaten from the tree
they wouldn't have known they were naked.
strange now to think perhaps we were
always meant to be this way.
bare. exposed.
without another soul to shame us
because they are like us, they are us.
wouldn't it be freeing to return home
here, on this earth?
yes, our bodies are temples, i believe.
it is and it always will be.
but we are all just children searching for
a place to be loved, vulnerable, ourselves
as we were designed.
and we were designed to be
open.

the art chose you for a reason.

when you look into the mirror,
callout everything you hate.
summon nothing but kindness.
wish it well into your bones.
remind yourself of magic.
dance with your reflection.
say "i love me."
repeat "i love me."

you are beautiful.
you are strong.
you are effervescent.
you are better than
enough.

give a woman flowers
and she'll smell them.
tell her that she is one,
and she'll *bloom*.

while there's fear, don't let it consume you.
the world is great and beautiful and
help can come from anywhere.
from people who've seen things and been places
as you've seen things and been places.
who know things you don't know and
don't know things you do.
so be kind.
choose to see the good in people.
and most of all choose to believe
they are with you and not against you.

you are your parts
and you are the sum of your parts.
when divided, none of you shall be lost.

i do not remember the millennium bug
or the day the earth stood silently still.
i have heard that people were fervently praying, repenting,
and hoping to cleanse their sins with blessed water.
they thought it was the end of the world
or the second coming of Christ.

i do not remember the millennium bug
or the day the earth stood silently still.
i was nearing six, and probably playing, eating, sleeping,
or some combination of the above.
eyes were fixed, hands were held, jobs were lost,
and nothing happened at all.
strange how even when you stop,
time is still moving.

all we know how to do is
make our journeys longer, not shorter.
but there is one straight path, and
if we stay with the light, we'll find it.

be so happy
with yourself
and with your work
that you are full
year-round.

you had the promise of being good.
like an untried dish from a recently opened restaurant
that sounded appealing on paper but fell a little short
on your taste buds and it took everything in you to
not let them see you gag as you wait for them to leave
so you can quietly go into the bathroom, spit it out
into a napkin, and rinse your mouth under the sink.

you had the promise of being good.
aside from rumors and bias.
if the world gave you a chance.
if you didn't act the way everyone else saw you.
*just because people wanted you to be the class clown
doesn't mean you had to be.*

you had the promise of being good.
the smile on your face was pure but
the look in your eyes was anything but.

i went to a poetry reading once.
the poet got to the last three lines and i sat there
and thought the poem had the promise of being good
there, just then.
but the rest barely scratched the surface.

and i think if we all have the promise of being good,
then there has to come a time when we fault ourselves
for not being, and demand more from the people we love because
we know that they're capable of it.

you are difficult to break.
that's why it hurts so much when you do.

the ways we fall asleep-
suddenly, unexpectedly.
our hearts dormant volcanoes once active-
as if we sat on our knees and had forgotten
we were sitting on it for hours
and it could still move.
forgetfulness and excitement:
the cause of all our troubles.
how could we sit so consistently
and not love the same length?

i turn to you when everything has gone dark.
i bring out the memory of you from the reserves
in the cabinets of my heart like
lanterns and candles when the lights go out.
the difference between you and candles is small but much.
the difference is you light up space
and you are no longer here.
your scent is there, but you are no longer here.
when i reach out my hand, i feel nothing,
get nothing from you when with a candle i burn.
the difference is you stick like wax, but
i can't see you.
the difference is i won't always have to
wait for hard rain for the power to go out.
i'll always want you, need you, remember you,
even when i don't want to.
what does it matter what the difference is
when i'm really listing similarities?
the similarity is i love and appreciate you,
but can only appreciate a candle.

it's easy to get wrapped up in things that can be taught.
like greatness.

in a world where we share the same dreams,
i hope you remember to be kind.
i hope you remember to passionate.

i've always been afraid of things smaller than me.
smaller things that run fast.
smaller things that are hard to catch.
smaller things that win at hide and seek.
spiders and centipedes and your love most of all
have replaced hair ties and phones and house keys-
things i lose that only come out when they want to.
i didn't know i lost you.
was it easy for you to watch?
me falling in love with you while your love was so small
i couldn't be sure you loved me at all.

this is what made me *stay*.

change doesn't happen overnight.
do you notice a difference in the sea after an earthquake?

soon enough you'll start seeing the same people every day
and though you don't know where they're going,
or where they've come from,
you love them anyway.

their desires become your wishes,
you've established a silent form of acknowledgment,
most times you nod, sometimes even smile.
and such is our cacophony.
coming and going. coming and going. coming and going.
and when they're gone, you'll know it.
you'll miss them and start to think,

we weren't really strangers after all.

you always found a reason to stay.
always found a reason to leave.
you were the anchor and the boat.
you wanted to be the sea.

softly, softly, everything will fall into place.
like raindrops into oceans.
like snowflakes into snow.
like ambiance.
like you.
softly, softly, everything that didn't have a place, will.
like courage.
like love.
like happiness.
and after it all, you won't be yourself again.
but darling, you were never supposed to.

the skin you've shed has already been replaced.
first, you survive. then you change.

"stand in front of the light. what do you see?"
"i see two different versions of me."
"which one is true?"
"neither."
"do you see why i cannot fall in love with you yet?"
"yes."

sometimes you won't have enough oxygen to
burn the fuel completely.
so while you'll mend some hearts,
you'll break some too.
while you'll have happy days,
you'll have sad ones too.
while you'll succeed a lot,
you'll fail a lot too.
and while you'll find your passions,
you'll have to work hard at them and know
when to let some of them go.
you don't become water without burning first.

i asked what you loved about the night and smiled when you talked about me.

the thing about growing is that you are never done.
your surroundings are ever-changing
and it can be a lot to process at once when you
don't even mean to absorb it.
but all i'm trying to say is:
you didn't ask to be a black hole,
and some things will never escape you,
but that doesn't mean you can't
make a light out of it.

i loved you like a wave;
gently, then suddenly,
i came over you.

when you start to put your hand in me,
like you're reaching for a cookie from a cookie jar,
remember you always have to ask for permission first.

remember when you get caught the taste won't be as sweet.

remember a snack will ruin your appetite.

whoever told you that you needed the sun to bloom
must have never loved a moonflower.

you are more of a fire than you think.
the gentle kind.
the kind that burns on a candle
and everyone gathers
to watch the air around it dance.
the kind that keeps everyone warm
on cold nights.
the kind that lights up paper trails
one by one by one.
the kind that the color of the flame
and intensity depends
on the matter.
that kind.
i'm so glad that fire is you.

we are taught that fragile is weak.
men should not cry, feel, or show emotions.
but a fragile little thing like you
has power to cut someone in two.

- like glass

how to make light out of darkness:
- pray.
- hope the wire of your feelings is strong enough to spark the wire of your imagination.
- express.
- forgive in time.
- contribute.
- make the most of it.
- and love with the fire of ten thousand exploding stars.

the first time they told you they loved you,
you refused to believe it.
it was one of those days where you were sad
and the sky was grey and
everywhere ached.
they would have said anything to
make you feel better.

the second time they told you they loved you,
you shook your head and smiled.
it was a placeholder to fill a moment of silence.
you knew better than to fall for that.

the third time they told you they loved you,
you had only begun to love yourself.
you couldn't believe anyone could
love you before you did,
but you should.

in case no one has told you,
it's okay to get used to this.
this love is for you.

if only we remembered how it felt like to let go,
instead of how much it hurt to do so,
we'd let go a little sooner.

look at how the waves
crash into the rocks
in order to rise and let
go.

steal your own heart.
believe in yourself.
do you not know of all the treasures buried
deep down inside you
waiting to be found?
you have searched far and long
and you will always be the most valuable thing.

so when you're feeling lost,
when you doubt your worth,
do not put your heart in other people.
do not put your hope.
there is no map to love,
but these treasures are ones
only you could know to look for.
and eventually you will learn,
eventually you will find your way,
eventually you will know who you are
in your purest form-
bright. soft. gold.

when a sense is lost,
the other senses work ten times harder
to compensate for the missing sense.
and just the same,
you will lose the sense of him or her
and find sense of yourself.

this i promise you.

know that the greatest root of all your sadness
comes from
traveling to the future
or
dwelling on the past.

you cannot control the water.
do not try to calm the shore.
an empty ship in a hurricane
is the most dangerous,
but you are not empty.
compared to the wind
the water is not your enemy.
head for a port.
(a hurricane hole)
let your walls drop like anchors
and hope.

there are 5-7 stages of grief
and you will go through all of them
but this is gospel:
this is yours but not alone.
there is room for more.
there is room for all of it here.

from the ones inside of us
to the ones outside of us,
we're all just trying to figure out
what pieces go together
and when.
so when you are tired,
remember to stay kind.
though you are a puzzle,
and they are a puzzle,
and everything is puzzling,
you deserve to be patient with yourself.
you deserve someone with enough patience
not to put you together
but to understand how you work.
understand how looks can be deceiving,
and understand your worth.

this weight you do not have to carry on your own.
your body is a map, not a sentence.

my first experience to the lack of respect
some men have for women
was when i was 22 and longing to be kissed
for the first time.

the man that came along was desperate too.
we left the party and ended up in his room.

he told me to feel how hard his dick was for me
as if by entering me
he would be made soft.

all i did was claim my religion.
for him, that was not enough.

it's easy to think that
people won't see you the way you see you,
but give yourself the opportunities you deserve.
because one day, someday soon, someone will see you
the way you see you and they'll wonder why
you didn't start sooner.

if all else fails
and you can't outrun the storm,
here is what you need to survive:
sea room and space to grow.
steering way to go forward.

if they let you go for no good reason,
they will regret it.
they would feel as if they were dying of thirst,
and will look for water and not find it.

that Sunday is the last i saw you.
my younger brother and i sat in pews and pointed out those
who don't normally appear for church on Sundays,
like those who don't normally take time to enjoy nature
until there is a rare celestial occurrence or the peak
of Cherry Blossom season.

Christmas.
Ash Wednesday.
The Week That Changed The World.
Easter.
i stared at you because you don't belong here.
you stared at me because i do.

just as it is your own, your experience can be my light.
just as it is my own, my experience can be your light.
and we will light the way.

the things meant for you will be like water.
enough to quench you.
enough to quench them too.

captain's coming.

you're the captain.

petal arms open up to hold you,
won't you produce honey?
this much has always been
up to you.

you are a living ceremony.
every day is a day to celebrate you
and the finer things in life.
my the wars you've won,
the loves you've had,
the loves you've lost
that were not meant for you.

it all comes down to this.
a feast in which you have set the table.
generously and kindly;
you are the guest, the host, the honoree.
gloriously made and blessed be.
don't you see how your feet have been carrying you
with your heart as the drum?
you have been dancing all along.
many lives, one song.
one beautiful earth as your home.

the ocean with all its rocks has never been
too much to follow.
too much to swim in.

when they mention you have too much going on,
too much to handle,
know it is a warning.

what is there for them to handle when
you are handling it?

they don't deserve your oceans if
they only want you more empty.

depend on yourself. be a sunflower.

do not forget to show yourself how beautiful you are.
he has touched you against your will like a
mimosa pudica, a touch-me-not,
and you have rightly folded into yourself.
but you were a grown flower before him,
and you can be after.
give yourself time and let your leaves fold out.
give yourself you.

one day life will stop giving you lemons and
you'll go looking for it in your own backyard.
from sad disposition, you'll find sad music.
the only way to share pain is through art.

the art becomes a culmination of things;
connections, interpretations, feelings.
it's what makes it timeless.
how you can look at it now and
be something.

if only you knew what it took for you to grow.
how much light you absorbed.
why your leaves turn yellow now,
and why to rise from the ash you must wear it.

as the dawn takes on a new day
and the air does the opposite of warming,
remember the hard times show you where you're at.
that if you see your true colors it means you broke.

look at the foliage happening before you
as longer days blend into shorter ones.
it has always been there waiting for you to rest.
waiting for you to turn to yourself to survive
the harshest of nights.
waiting for you to know your worth.

once you were a kid behind a lemonade stand
waiting for someone to see it.
but my, how you've grown.

He gave you wings but *you* chose to fly.

you don't have to be this heavy thing to break things down.
a breath can be mighty enough to blow a candle
and you are a thousand breaths from a thousand lifetimes.
you can move mountains.
move mountains.
you won't always know what you'll leave in your wake, but
you could be love too and it'll be enough.
it is enough.

anything you put your heart and soul into,
no matter the outcome,
is not a waste of time.

loving you was like loving fireworks.
there was anticipation before magic,
silence before loud,
darkness before color,
hello before goodbye,
and every piece of being i wanted for us
come to die.

loving you was settling.
settling for brief instead of lasting,
gray instead of black,
pretty instead of beautiful,
when i should have known the difference.

loving you was a reminder
that i do not need a love like this.
i do not need a love like this.

to those that try to steal your thunder,
show them they gave you an opportunity to shine.

i am realizing how easy it is to be two things at once.
how rain can pour on one side of the sidewalk,
but the other is clear as day.
how i can be in love with you and not.
how freeing it is and how i should not be sorry for it.

home was a pitiful static.
dreams of leaving went in and out of tune like
dreams from those who constantly wish to travel but
didn't have the matter.
i mimicked a fever.
longing struck like lightning.
i waited.
"it won't be like this forever"
was my excuse to stay.
to tolerate things that
shouldn't have been tolerated.

this is my moment of silence
for the life i could have had
if i didn't grow up in a nineteenth-century home.
a home where men were guests and
women had to serve,
keep their legs closed,
never go out with a man alone.
couldn't drink except in church,
couldn't wear shorts in 90 degree weather,
had to pay attention to figure,
had to wear sweaters to cover up flaws,
pimples and stretch marks,
pimples and stretch marks,
on backs and arms.

this is my moment for
all the art i could have created
if i made it out long ago and
all the art i created when i didn't.

taking them back
will show you who you are
as a person,
and leaving them
will show you how strong
you've become.

if there is one thing we were meant to share,
it is the braiding of the hair.
my mother, her mother, her mother's mother
sitting with their daughters placed
in the folds of their laps,
with straight backs,
as silk soft fine hair,
coarse hair is spun.
as they weave truth.
as pain is sacrificed for beauty
in the black girl, white girl, mixed girl,
as love becomes strength that we pick up and wear
out into the world,
yes, i am that woman.
yes, i am that girl.

when you lace your fingers in her hair,
remember this.

when you abuse her and grab her by the hair,
remember this.

no amount of love that has been passed down
from generations
can be undone.

yes, we are women.
yes, we are one.

if the love has nowhere to go, let it stay with you.

after he leaves you,
you'll think that you cannot love anymore
because you have no more love left in you.
but the truth is,
there is so much love left in you.
you just have to relearn how to give it
and be open to receiving it.

love, hate, fear, or hope, you are responsible for
the things you carry into this world.

to fall in line.
that's what it feels like to be women.
we seal our lips,
never raise our voice above a whisper,
sit with our legs closed.
womanhood was required and playfulness was privileged.
we became women long before we became girls.
walk, don't run.
sit still, just smile.
bleed each month but never show it.
within every blossomed woman is a budding girl
and mine will know to step out of
line.

let your troubled waters be filled with salt.
it will become so dense that you will not sink.

the bees approach the flower
in search of nectar and pollen.
sucking and chewing once found
long enough to make honey.
somehow, even the bees know
the longer you sit on something
the more it will be sweet.

to be free is to know the importance of yourself.
you are worth more than all the things that tie you down.
never stop fighting for you.

these are powerful words:
yes, no, can, can't, do, don't,
should, would, could, is, is not,
and here's what else i know-
soldier, the horizon is not a line.
unleash the victory you had
in you all along.
think positive. hope.
the hell in your city
will last as long as you let it.
stand straight and breathe
heavenly fire.

love. not because it makes you happy,
but because it sets you free.

i know what it's like when your mind is the loudest and
doubt creeps in through the windows like a breeze.
it's like all the light disappears in its wake and
it becomes easy to get lost in the room you're in.

you wonder how you got here.
gone are the days when you knew yourself
inside and out.
knew every turn in every hallway.
could name every famous painting in history that lined
its walls and who made it, even though you studied it
your whole life.

you forgot they started in a place like you or i.
not knowing what they were doing but
having the courage to try.
they were kind.
kept failing and sharing.
paying the price and calling it sacrifice.
didn't sleep, couldn't sleep, didn't eat.
all they wanted was to make things for themselves.

isn't that what made them great?
isn't that what makes you great?
you have done so much good.
your failure is your success.
there is no doubt in my mind that you belong.
belong there standing with the best of the best.
in that room; the grand hall.
you have never been an imposter.
you have always been an artist.

what makes you, you is what you make for you.

as the month goes on
and the leaves change and fall,
the tree from which they fell is
riddled with scars.
it knows it can't heal,
so it seals that place to
protect what's left.

a year from now it would have bloomed.
rich with green to start anew.
and after all is said and done,
if it can survive, so can you.
you are healthy even with your
thousand wounds.

hold on to just enough of yourself to feel something.

at times it feels like all you are good for is
letting things hurt you.
that since you are made of water,
you should be water.
cast aside like ocean tides.
emotional.

when others tell you they admire how
strong you are, soft you are, smart you are,
you laugh because you don't feel it.
you feel weak, heavy, stupid.
it's hard to see that when they are talking of your strengths,
they are talking about what you are made of.
they are.

you are /you are made of / you are made of all /
you are made of all the light you cannot see /
all the light you can see / the dust that dances in between /
-beams- / you are made of clay / smaller pieces /
smaller pieces of those that came before you /
smaller pieces of things that have yet to come /
you are made of strings / heartstrings /
can you feel your heart beat?
you are made of art.

but though you are a work of art,
you are human too.
and what you are made of and how you feel
do not have to be one and the same.

your burial is your rise.
allow yourself to burn,
let the flavors of you
come alive.
you are made
for something greater
than yourself.

such power you hold.
being the only one able to love all of you when
the skin you've lost is gone for good.

the opposite of darkness is a call to action.
o's do not always follow x's,
but dark periods are followed by the movement of a sea,
this sea is women, this sea is me.

poetic as we are,
the only metaphor you should look for is metamorphosis.
i will become the demand and the supplier.
if i don't get the love i want, i will make the love i need.
whistle all you want, i will blow off steam.
i wasn't given a raise, but i will show you what i can do.
me too is from me to you.
me too is from me to you.

no matter the circumstance,
you must not let them
take your salt
and leave you *bitter*.

it is a struggle.
finding a representation of yourself
in shows or plays or movies you love.
your absence says much without meaning to say much.

is it a struggle,
and still, you must create the things you wish to see.

here's an interesting fact about fireflies:
not all produce light.
it was originally thought that
photic emission was the sole factor
for attraction and mating,
but flies that fly during the day
prove this isn't the case.
science has narrowed it down to pheromones-
while bioluminescence aids in the flashiness of courtship
it's not needed to mate.
i guess what i'm trying to say is:

you don't have to have the same experiences
to know the same love.

someday blessings will reign from within you and upon you.
one after another they'll come and
they'll wonder how a human could ever resemble a
meteor shower.

love is so out of this world,
i want to build a rocketship inside me.
take you with me to the top so
everyone can know a chemistry
so strong and universal as
sisterhood.

in the midst of it all, the pain and suffering,
you wonder if it is possible to bear fruit
without dying in the process.
there is so much you've undergone.
everything you've worked for seems pointless.
everything you've worked for gets smaller and smaller
until there is nothing but it, there is no more you.
you're outnumbered in a battle you think you cannot win.

i know those moments.
those moments where pain overwhelms
the sound of His voice;
the most natural light of them all.
the hardest thing about faith is that
"the spirit is willing and the flesh is weak."
without belief, we are lost.

i know those moments.
i know them all too well.
so well i know that though love is a poison,
the greatest of them all,
it will not kill us because it lives in us.
all it takes is for someone to bring it out.

and the cure is what we forged
when we established our bond.
what we survived together.

you poured
yourself
into them.
your body. your skin.
all of you.
suffered.

- the war is over (if you want)

lessons we can learn from nature:

if you watch a caterpillar from start to finish,
you'd notice it melt almost completely.
what's left in the chrysalis is nothing but memories
and parts of it that have long stopped growing.
it's from these parts
it will form again and grow the wings you see.
proof that no matter how dim, light in darkness exists.

the take away is this:

see how the caterpillar is responsible for
all of its shedding?
molting several times before the last.
in every stage it finds a home and
there is so much love around this.

bareness has never been a weakness.

don't let what you have suffer because of
what you don't have.

if there is anything we should learn,
it's that no flame is eternal.
no matter how dark it gets,
there is hope.
near every black hole,
there is a horizon.
a sun is not too far behind.

it is times like these we should
draw the line.
figure out what matters most.
see the pause as a chance to realign.
"life begins outside of your comfort zone."

after this, i hope you never settle for anything.
do everything worth doing with a smile.
find love under this infinite sky.
and make sure who you love knows it.

remind yourself a thousand times if you have to:
the battle means nothing if you're not holding the pen.

your voice is the most expensive gift you can give
and it is made to crack.
do not stand down.
do not hide your voice.
now you must take shape like art,
like pottery repaired with gold.
your flaws make you.
and though there is much you do not know,
you are meant to hold all that is wrong in the world
and make it good.
make it good.

words are waiting at the cusp of your tongue.
write them.

Acknowledgments

first and foremost,
i would like to thank God for blessing me with this talent.
for allowing me to cultivate the relationships i have in my life;
past, present, and future.
second,
to my best friend Jessie,
who puts up with reading my work:
still offering suggestions even when her brain is fried.
i love you Tot.
third,
to my writing professors.
especially Lucas Southworth.
you always believed in me. thank you.
fourth,
to Amanda Torroni and Tyler Kent White.
your poetry challenges pushed me to be a better writer.
fifth,
to those special writers that have shared this space with me.
your talent is unparalleled.
last,
to those of you that have been
with me on my journey.
it means the world to me.

Honorable Mentions

Rupi Kaur, Kendal Marie,
Kevin T. Norman, Edie Garpne,
Daniel Salgado, Katherine Victoria,
Emma Roberts,
and **my family**.

whether this stays on your shelf or in your heart,
thank you for reading.

Made in the USA
Las Vegas, NV
31 August 2021